T0208327

Warrior Spirit

A Journey of Reflection, Redemption, and Recovery

LISA ALLEN THOMPSON

authorHOUSE®

AuthorHouse™
1663 Liberty Drive
Bloomington, IN 47403
www.authorhouse.com
Phone: 833-262-8899

Published by AuthorHouse   04/17/2023

ISBN: 979-8-8230-0609-5 (sc)
ISBN: 979-8-8230-0607-1 (hc)
ISBN: 979-8-8230-0608-8 (e)

Library of Congress Control Number: 2023906761

Print information available on the last page.

A percentage of all sales from this book will be donated to non-profit organizations that empower and protect the circle of life and promote non-violence, also mental health issues and healthy living.

With love and appreciation, thank you!

CONTENTS

ACKNOWLEDGEMENTS

It was the early summer of 2017, I was in a hospital triage room, twisted in fetal position, broken physically, mentally, emotionally, spiritually, and financially, with no desire to survive. Having had more than my share of loss, abandonment issues, trauma and heartache, I was done! I had bore the proverbial last straw! I was held for observation with a crisis counselor for just a few hours. Being in social services myself I knew the drill. I faked my best presentation of normality and calm, got myself released, with full intent on going through with my plan, totally suicidal.

By the grace of divine intervention I am still here!

With counseling and support groups I discovered my demons and brokenness was not a defect in my character, but years of unhealed hurt and heartbreak. It was a rude awakening and revelation to take responsibility and accept I was the result of my own low self-worth. The only one I can change is myself! I am Blessed to have many friends, and some family, who held me up, held space for me, and held love and hope…I would learn to love myself.

So began my recovery!

In addition to rebuilding my life, I also began to resurrect my creativity. I have been writing poetry and song lyrics most of my life and utilized this talent during my search of self! It was a Monday night that I shuffled in to my first Open Mic. I quietly and discreetly took a seat in the back row and just observed. Within a few weeks I began sharing my poetry and song lyrics, and it was there, my creative heart and soul was reborn! The ripple effect of becoming part of this creative community was meeting other poets, songwriters, bands and musicians, who I now know as friends! Writing and music has always been my celebration and solace, and I hope my creativity will bring celebration and solace to others too. It is with grace and gratitude I give thanks to The Buttonwood Tree Performing Arts

Center, and director: Ms. Ann-Marie Cannata McEwen. Also, forever love and light, to my friends: Ms. Terri Lachance and Rob DeSorbo.

My creativity continued to be a source of preservation as was exploring my spirituality. As a little girl I loved being in the woods. I would gather rocks, twigs, flowers, and water, and make altars and small sanctuaries. Sticks served as drumsticks for making music on flat rocks. Little did I know then, drums would be my passion, and I was a free spirit in training! Now as a grown-up I discovered another sanctuary where I would be free to be me. At a nature sanctuary I met a group of people also exploring spirituality through guided mediation and group discussions. I learned to go within through meditation and trust the journey. Trust is a huge issue for me, so finding this place of serenity with kindred spirits was a gift! I began to understand or at least have an awareness that everything does happen for a reason. We do learn from both the lessons and blessings of life. The path will present itself and the answers will be revealed in divine timing. I am learning to let go of the illusion of control and allow life to manifest according to plan. I feel blessed to share this pilgrimage with other beings at this beautiful nature sanctuary…and there is also music… and drums!!!

I am so very thankful for The Sanctuary and for the dedication and love of its directors: Mr. Justin Good and Ms. Jen Taylor. Justin for your guidance and support at our meditations and discussion groups. Jenny forever grateful for your song: "A Walk Is A Living Poem." You are both blessings to all of us who venture there.

My journey continued with an additional modality of natural health… Sound Meditation. Sound Meditation as I understand it is a guided mediation with a practitioner who utilizes gongs, crystal bowls, chimes, and drums. The vibrational sounds are said to remove blockages in our body and aid in using sound to clear your mind and deepen meditation. It has proven to be effective in physical health, mental health, and spiritual health. My first experience with sound meditation was unsettling! The vibrational sounds and deep meditation can bring awareness to many emotions! With continued practice I learned to work through them. With patience and guidance from my practitioner I learned to sit with my emotions. I learned to sit with it, process it, and let it go…and just breathe in and breath out. Sound Mediation remains an amazing experience for me and is part of my holistic health routine and conscious healing. I owe a debt of gratitude to Tracy Kroll of The Sound Retreat and his presence along my journey.

It was a dark, long, and hard climb from rock bottom, but there were some powerful guiding lights of love:

LIFE SISTERS: Heather St.Clair, Catherine Flynn, Joanie Rich, Sue Cruz, Barb Russ, Deb Straiton, Wendy Von Egidy, Corinne Thompson, and Pam Nelson.

SISTERFRIENDS: Emily Masters, Nancy Fraga, Hedy Watrous, Lee-Ann Lovelace, Lori Clark, Gayle Kimball, Karen Walmsley, Jude Rittenhouse, Ruth Parker, and Maureen Ward.

SOULSISTERS: Terri Lachance and Melissa Charity

MUSIC…music heals! DRUMS…the heartbeat of the body and soul!

Boldly and with meekness, and the grace of humility, from my heart and soul, I share with you, my warrior spirit.

Love & Light, Lisa

Dedicated to my Grandchildren:
Rebecca Elizabeth
&
Luke Mark
May you always have a song in your heart and peace in your soul.

Special thanks and tribute to the memory of:
Tom Laughlin and Delores Taylor

For the movie Billy Jack and your dedication and legacy of being true humanitarians and advocates of social justice. You made a profound influence on my life back in the 1970's, and I carry it with me still today! You fueled my advocacy that each of us can make this world a better place and sharing through our own creativity heals ourselves and others. Although you are both in the spirit world now you cemented a cause to believe in for my generation and beyond!

"Regardless of affluence or tutelage, I believe the true measure of success, a true humanitarian, and decent human being…remains a commoner at heart and soul, for the every day hero."

~ Lisa Allen Thompson

Reflection

BAD-ASS LADY
Dedicated to: Elizabeth Ann Sinclair Allen

I inherited my love of music and creative writing from my Mom. She was an American Bandstand, Black & White TV, AM Radio, teenage Mom. She was barely sixteen years old when I was born, "we grew up together, my Mama-Child and me."

She was quite the rebel! When she saw injustice in the world or community, she would write letters to the editors of the local newspapers, and also did not shy away from writing letters to her Representatives, Senators, and other applicable powers that be!

Mom gave little regard to hypocrites or phonies, and if you knew her, you knew where you stood with her, good, bad, or indifferent. If she had a Manhattan in hand it was most likely vocalized a bit louder and bit more explicit.

We lived in a small rural town that wasn't without its scandals and gossip. She always joked she was going to write a book titled: "Around and About Town," and stated she was going to make her big money from the people who would pay her NOT to publish it!

She loved music! Our house was always filled with music! Putting records on the stereo and dancing around the livingroom and kitchen are some of my favorite memories.

I inherited my love of music and creative writing from my Mom! She was one helluva lady…and make no mistake she was a lady…one bad-ass lady!

My definition of Bad-Ass Lady: A woman who doesn't depend on the opinion of others to validate herself. One that shows both bravery and compassion.

LITTLE GIRL DREAMS

When I grow- up I want to be
A writer of some kind,
A lyricist, a poet, or maybe both
I just love to make words rhyme.

WHY, WHEN, WHAT, WHERE, WHO?

Who am I?
Where am I going?
What am I trying so hard to do?
When will I know?
Why does it matter?
Why, when, what, where, who?

SOMEWHERE

Somewhere…
Between,
The laughter and the tears,
Somewhere…
Between,
The raindrops and the sunbeams,
Is a rainbow of truth…
A hope…
And a promise…
To believe in,
And live out-
Our dreams.

UNLOCK THE DOOR

The road that leads to what you want
Is right outside your door,
It's the key that opens up the lock
That you're still searching for.

Happiness is right around the corner
With dreams ready to come true,
And peace of mind is also there
All waiting there…for you.

The road is already at your door
And the door opens at your command-
Because the key that fits in to the lock
Is right in your own hand.

A FREE WORLD

I believe we can make a world
Where all people are really free,
If everyone would try together
All people...like you and me.

Where everywhere peace could be known
Where we can put an end to war,
Where love walks ahead of hate
On all lands...shore to shore.

Where happiness stays ahead of sad
Where laughter is heard more than a cry,
Where trust and honesty could be known by all
And live together...side by side.

Where people would look and really see
Where they would listen and really hear,
Where all colors and sexual orientations agree
And there was no such thing as fear.

I believe we can make a world
Where all people are really free,
If everyone would try together
All people...like you and me.

BEAUTIFUL DREAMER

Make a wish upon a star
Wishes do come true,
What you put out to the universe
Comes around and back to you.

Dream, you beautiful dreamer
Dreams do come true,
Embrace the vision of your intention
It's already got a hold on you.

What you put out to the universe
Comes around and back to you,
So, make a wish upon a star
Because wishes do come true.

Embrace the vision of your intention
It's already got a hold on you,
So, dream you beautiful dreamer
Because dreams do come true...

Make a wish upon a star
Beautiful dreamer that you are.

FLOWER CHILD

A part of me will always be
A die hard flower child,
The times keep right on changing
But they haven't changed my style.

I still believe peace has a chance
And there's a better way than war,
If we all would try together
All of us, rich and poor.

I still don't care for phonies
The in crowd or being hip,
I don't like being lied to or about
And I don't care for hypocrites.

I still listen to music every day
And I still dig poetry,
Country, Rock, Folk, Motown-
All groovy cool to me!

The times keep right on changing
But they haven't changed my style,
A part of me will always be
A die hard flower child.

A WAY OF LIFE

It's a gamble in the morning
It's a gamble noon and night,
It's a gamble month to month to month
It's just a way of life!

Borrow from Peter to pay Paul
Now Peter's broke again,
Next week Paul pays Peter back
And the spinning wheel spins!

I bet the rent against the car loan
I bet the phone against the lights,
I bet the deposit against the checks
And with luck it turns out alright!

Borrow from Peter to pay Paul
Now Peter's broke again,
Next week Paul pays Peter back
And the spinning wheel spins!

It's a gamble in the morning
It's a gamble noon and night,
It's a gamble month to month to month
It's just a way of life!

LITTLE GIRL DREAMS
(Packed Away)

When I grew up I dreamed I'd be
A writer of some kind,
A lyricist, a poet, or maybe both
I just loved to make words rhyme.

Then adulthood came way too soon
I was thrown in to the mainstream,
A real job, a home, and family
Washed away my little girl dreams.

Packed away in my closet
Were notebooks of my rhymes,
Forsaken dreams now dreaming me
Good-bye little girl dreams of mine.

EVERYTHING

(For my daughter: Judi Lee)

Everything to some people
Would be a mansion on the hill,
Gold and silver, and possessions
And rolling in dollar bills.

But money can't buy happiness
Or give you a big hug,
Or buy you peace of mind
And it sure can't buy you love!

Everything is a place called home
However humble it may be,
Filled with trust and happiness
And loving someone who loves me.
Add to that a little someone
The pitter patter of little feet,
Who looks at me all aglow-
And says: "I love you Mommie."
Being satisfied with your work
Whatever it may be,
The love of family and love of friends
That's everything to me!

Everything to some people
Would be a mansion on the hill,
Gold and silver, and possessions
And rolling in dollar bills.

But money can't buy happiness
Or give you a big hug,
Or buy you peace of mind
And it sure can't buy you love!

CHILDREN

The most precious thing on this earth
Is a little child,
Bless them for their honesty
Each unique in their own style.

Bless each and every one
The meek and the mild,
Bless each and every one
The reckless and the wild,
Bless each and every one
Each and every little child.

They're not afraid to be themselves
Bless the innocence of their tears and their smiles
The most precious thing on this earth
Is a little child.

LAUGH AND LAUGH AND LAUGH

When I was a teenager I was a bit of a wild child! I WAS a wild child! Not in a criminal way, but, a freedom fighter, pot smoking, Boones Farm Strawberry Wine, let's party, rock and roll, turn the music up loud, kind of wild child! Every time I got in trouble (you could count on me to be grounded every other weekend!) my Mom would say: "I hope some day you have a daughter just like you!" In response, my smartass wild child self would sarcastically, laugh and laugh and laugh!

Fast forward…a few years later…

When my daughter was three years old we got her a Hotwheel bicycle for her birthday. She couldn't wait to try it out! At her birthday party with friends and family in attendance she took it for its first spin. So we all watched, as she rolled it to the top of our hill out behind our house, jumped on, and down she came full speed. Singing at the top of lungs, she hit the gravel driveway, grabbed the brake, spun a 360 degree doughnut, and yelled: "YE-HA!"

My Mother looked over at me, with the same smartass look I gave to her a few years ago, and laughed and laughed and laughed!

IF YOU'RE LISTENING NOW
(Divorce)

You look at me, but you don't see me
I'm talking to you, but you don't hear,
I've givin' my all, my everything
What to do now is perfectly clear.

I needed you to love and believe in me
But you turned a deaf ear to my songs,
You never cared about my music or rhymes
If you're listening now…I'm gone!

It's been a long time coming
But I can't keep pretending to be someone I'm not,
If all is fair in love and war
I lost every battle I fought.

I needed you to love and believe in me
But you turned a deaf ear to my songs,
You never cared about my music or rhymes
But, if you're listening now…I'm gone!

LIFE IS KINDA FUNNY

Around sixty-eight or sixty-nine
In the prime of my youth,
My parents didn't understand me
They just weren't "in the groove."
Barefooted and in faded jeans
With flowers in my hair,
They thought I was "a hippie"
I thought that they were "square."
I'd tell them in plain English
"Man, stop being so uptight!"
"Just hang loose and keep cool,"
"Everything is like, outta sight!"

But they didn't understand me
Because as I walked away,
I heard my Dad say to my Mom-
"What the hell did she just say?"

I just really blew their minds
With the things I'd do and say,
And I knew someday when I had kids
I'd be so cool, and not that way!

Now here I am all grown up
With a daughter of my own,
The parent of a teenager
And it shakes me to the bone!
She wears wild colored baggy jams
And long tee shirts to her knees,
She has these clip things in her hair
And Reeboks on her feet.
So I could better understand
Her generation and lifestyle,
I asked if we could sit and talk
And so, we "rapped" awhile.

She said, "Mom, I'll give it to you straight,"
"I don't know what you worry about?"
"My life is totally very awesome,"
"So, like really…just chill out!"

You know life is kinda funny
Because as she walked away,
I laughed out loud as I thought-
"What the hell did she just say?"

LIFE IS KINDA MORE FUN

The year is now 2010! My grown-up daughter has a teenager of her own! My daughter was a child of the mid 1990's, so another generation arrives.

Her daughter, my Granddaughter, is all excited about a school dance that is coming up. They are all going to go in costume, dressed up as old rock n' rollers. When we asked her who she might go dressed up as, she answered: "I am thinking Cyndi Lauper!" The look on my daughters face was priceless!

Oh yes! The golden age of rock n' roll! So very long ago!

Side note: For the record…all three of us LOVE Cyndi Lauper!

TECNO-CHALLENGED

Soooo…my eleven year old granddaughter just received an Ipod for her birthday. She's sitting at the computer "downloading" and "shuffling" and slicin' and dicin', and everything else the technological modern marvel of recording equipment does! (?)

I remember when I was approximately the same age (No! I didn't walk to school in the snow, uphill both ways! That was the generation before me!) I was thrilled to get my Transistor Radio! You could take your music anywhere you wanted to go…almost! You see getting your Transistor Radio to come in was another story! Kind of like the first cell phones: "Can you hear me now?" Walk around, spin in circle, "can you hear me now?" You walked around until you found that spot, that area, where you actually heard music coming from the radio! You could take it anywhere! No cord. No electrical outlet, just charged batteries! You just had to be able to move, north…south…east…west…until your Transistor Radio played music! Then, there you stayed or danced around listening to your favorite radio stations! So, this new technological modern marvel of recording equipment the Ipod is truly amazing to this Grannie, who appears is tecno-challenged!

Also, I have a three year old grandson. At this point in his life his favorite modern marvel of technology is Satellite TV! One day while my grandson and I were watching Satellite TV, he asked me to "DVR" his favorite show. D-V-R? "Record it Grannie!" OK, shouldn't be that hard I guess. WRONG! You see, Grannie "scrambled" the Satellite TV, and had no clue how to "unscramble" Satellite TV! Now we have no TV! Tecno-challenged!

When Grannie was a little girl TV was not complicated! If you wanted to watch a TV show besides the one that was on the screen, you had one option, turn the big dial with all the numbers on it right or left, and have your pick of five or six other shows, or go back and watch the one you were watching! If you wanted the sound softer or louder, you turned the little dial to the right for louder, or to the left for softer! If the picture wasn't clear, that indicated you needed more tin foil on the antenna's, or wiggle and move them around until the picture was clear!

Grannie is from the wonder years! The good ol' days of LP's and 45's on vinyl, Reel to Reel Recording, 8 Tracks, Black and White TV, and Transistor Radios! Oh, and my most treasured RCA Victrola! You know what? I really don't mind being tecno-challenged! It was a simpler time… those good ol' days!

SURVIVAL

I remember walking into the kitchen in the house I grew up in and telling my Mom I was running away from home! I was running away from home because her and Dad didn't understand me and they wouldn't let me live the way I wanted to! I was approximately twelve or thirteen and had life figured out. My Mom packed me a care package of a tuna sandwich, chips, and a thermos of Kool-Aid. (In my Monkees lunchbox!) I went to my bedroom and packed the essentials! Besides clothing and food, I needed some LP's and 45's, my portable RCA Victrola, and some paper and pens to write home about all my adventures living life my way! Out the door I went!

Away I go! Living life my way! I went to one of my favorite areas, across the brook, up the hill, to the big rock. (You could see the house from there!) I encountered my first hardship within minutes. There was no place to plug in my RCA Victrola! I was NOT prepared for this kind of hardship! Storms, wild animals, invasion of space aliens...but NO MUSIC? There is no survival for me with no music!

I decided to sing! I sang my little heart out for my free self and free world. I was free to live my life my way! Except...there was no place to plug in my RCA Victrola.

Also, where the hell is the search team? The news crews, a helicopter? My family doesn't even miss me? It has been hours and they haven't heard from me! Don't they wonder how my life of living life my way turned out? It's getting dark out now too! Dark enough the lights just went on in the house. And there is no place to plug in my RCA Victrola!

That's what I remember the most about my first taste of freedom! Living life my way! There was no place to plug in my RCA Victrola and I couldn't survive without music! A mere child, but, I already knew...to survive life my way...I needed my music!

LITTLE GIRL DREAMS REVISTED

When I was young, a little girl
I wanted to be a writer of some kind,
A songwriter, a poet, or maybe both
I just loved to make words rhyme.

Packed away deep in my closet
Out of sight but not out of mind,
Laid to rest my little girl dreams
And notebooks of my rhymes.

After several years and growing old
I unpacked those notebooks of mine,
And reflected on those little girl dreams
Picked up my pen and wrote some rhymes.

When I grew- up I dreamed I'd be
A writer of some kind,
A songwriter, a poet, maybe both
All grown-up I think it's time.

Redemption

DEAR MOM & DAD

As far back as I remember
I was your rebel one,
I had a mind of my own
And my own ways to get things done.
And lately I've been thinking
About the years gone by,
The people and the places
And the way I feel inside.
I remember my support of social justice
And the times I marched for peace,
Freedom, Equality, and Human Rights
Standing up for my beliefs.
Life moves swiftly onward
Things change and some stay the same,
Me, I have gone through many changes
But my rebel ways remain.
As far back as I remember
Had my own ways to get things done,
So I guess I'll always and forever-
Be your rebel one!

DEATHBED GOOD-BYE

In Memory of my Mom: Elizabeth Ann Sinclair Allen

Mom…I'm sorry for my wild years
I know I let you down,
I wish I turned out better and made you proud
Instead, I screwed up all around.

Remember the time you searched my room
And found my "homemade cigarettes?"
And the time I took your car and ran away?
Mom…I was such a brat!

Remember nothing ever scared me?
And if it did, I hid it well,
I'd stand toe to toe with the devil
And tell him go to hell!

Mom…I'm not as strong as people think
And I don't know how to ask for help,
Because I've always been the rebel!
Promise you won't tell?

She answered:
I'm not worried about you little girl
You'll make it, you always do,
You always land on your feet
I know I can count on you!
So…don't go changing on me now
Your rebel ways will get you through,
I love you…my rebel child
And I've always been proud of you.

Mom…I love you too!

RECORDING STUDIO

When I was a little girl I played recording studio! Most little girls were playing House, Nurse, Mommie, playing with their baby dolls. I played recording studio! I would be in my room with my RCA Victrola, my tape recorder, and all my favorite bands on vinyl…and my room transformed into a recording studio!

"Come over baby whole lot of shakin' going on…"
I would have loved being in Memphis, Tennessee at Sun Records in the good old days of rock n' roll. Elvis! Jerry Lee Lewis! Johnny Cash! Carl Perkins! Love those rockin' cats!

"Just one more mornin'…I had to wake up with the blues…"
Muscle Shoals Sound Studio! I would have given anything to be at Muscle Shoals back in the day, especially with Duane Allman!
"…wake up momma…turn your lamp down low…"
Can you imagine? Imagine sitting in jamming with the likes of: Duane Allman, Lynyrd Skynyrd, Wilson Pickett, Aretha Franklin, Joe Cocker, Tony Jo White, Johnny Rivers, Bonnie Bramlett…Melissa Etheridge! The Rolling Stones recorded at Muscle Shoals! Oh, if I could have been there!
"…wild horses couldn't drag me away…"

If you asked me to name my favorite recording of date…I could probably narrow it down to a top fifty…but I guess the first to come to mind, is one by one of my all time favorite bands- Aerosmith. "Honkin' On Bobo!" American music at best, by an American band at best! At The Boneyard!

When I was a little girl I played recording studio.

TOUR VAN

It was another Saturday in a small town of the USA, and my rock band and me were getting ready for another world tour!

Off we'd go…through the pasture…across the bridge over the brook… to the dirt road…and across the cow lot…where our tour van waited. To most people it was an old rusted out station wagon with wheels sunk down into the earth, that time had long forgotten. But to me and my rock band it was a tour van!

We went all around the world in that van! The tours waxed and waned depending on who in the neighborhood wanted to be in my rock show that day. Sometimes I was a solo act, sometimes I had an opening act, and sometimes we were a regular rock fest like Woodstock! We played with all the great rock bands of the 60's.

Yeah…we drove anywhere we wanted to go and rocked the world!

We were young and free and believed in our dreams. In that tour van we could go anywhere, do anything, and be anybody we wanted to be!

Sometimes…I wish I could go back…and walk through the pasture, across the bridge over the brook, to the dirt road, and across the cow lot…to my tour van.

SMALL TOWN BLUES

I wonder what life would be like now
If in my younger days,
I had up and left here
Would I be better off today?

I wonder what would've happened?
I wonder what could've been?
I wonder if I should've gone?
Got the small town blues again.

Got the small town blues again
The would've...could've...should've
And the way it might've been-
If I had it to do over
I wonder what might've been
Right now I got the small town blues-
Got the small town blues, again.

I don't mean to sound down hearted
Because it ain't been all that bad,
And when I really take a look around
I'm thankful for what I have.

I have a family that I care about
I have the love of many friends,
I have a roof above my head
It's just the small town blues again.

Got the small town blues again
The would've...could've...should've
And the way it might've been-
If I had it to do over
I wonder what might've been
Right now I got the small town blues-
Got the small town blues, again.

EIGHT TRACKS & SIX PACKS

Just got a country oldies CD
And I'm singing along,
My old country top twenty
Are now my good old days songs.

We were eight tracks and six packs
And parties 'til dawn,
Man, where did it go?
Time sure did move along!

Remember hayfield keggers
And tailgate parties in trucks?
Sharin' smokes, shots of homebrew
Boones Farm Wine in paper cups?
Remember bonfires and camping
And "the rope" at the lake?
The Marbledale Pub
The secret make-out place?
Remember sing-alongs at parties
Before karoke became a thing?
Dancing in the livingroom to records
Talking out on the porch swing?

We were eight tracks and six packs
And parties 'til dawn,
Man, where did it go?
Time sure did move along!

Just got a country oldies CD
And I'm singing along,
My old country top twenty
Are now my good old days songs.

GIVIN' LOVE AND GETTIN' USED

Feelings inside me
I won't talk about-
Built a wall 'round my heart
To keep love out!

Still I keep searching
For what I'm scared to find,
A true love, a soulmate
A real love like mine.

I know I have it all to give
I just don't have it all to lose,
I'm down to my last broken heart
Givin' love and gettin' used.

Still I keep searching
For what I'm scared to find,
A true love, a soulmate
A real love like mine.

To share feelings inside me
I dare talk about-
To take down the walls
Built to keep love out!

I know I have it all to give
I just don't have it all to lose,
I'm down to my last broken heart
Givin' love and gettin' used.

I'm down to my last broken heart...
No more givin' love and gettin' used.

LOVE SONG

Some day I'll write a love song
Not another love gone wrong song,
When Mr. Right comes along
I'll write a true love song.

I'll free myself from this fortress
And hide away no more-
I'll release my shackled heart
Lay down my shield and sword.
The protection I once needed
For the shattered heart I bore-
Will once again feel safe
With faith in love restored.

Some day I'll write a love song
Not another love gone wrong song,
When Mr. Right comes along
I'll write a true love song.

When I feel safe once again
When faith in love is restored-
No more protection I will need
For the shattered heart I bore.
When I release my shackled heart
And lay down my shield and sword-
I'll free myself from this fortress
And hide away no more.

Some day I'll write a love song
Not another love gone wrong song,
When Mr. Right comes along
I'll write a true love song.

ACCOMPANY ME

Come along, sing my song
Come accompany me-
I'll let you be you
If you let me be me!

I'm a free spirit
I'll always be-
So don't clip my wings
Come fly with me.

Can you come along, sing my song?
Can you accompany me?
I'll let you be you
If you let me be me!

The time is now
Heart and soul tellin' me-
To do those someday things
And be who you wanted to be!

Can you come along, sing my song?
Can you accompany me?
I'll let you be you
If you let me be me!

Come along, sing my song...
Come accompany me.

KEEP ON WALKIN'

I'm lookin' for the real deal
Someone to be a lover and a friend,
I'll walk the line if you will too
And if you can't, well then you can-

Stop eye ballin' and your gawkin'
And I ain't fallin' for sweet talkin'
If you're not in it for the long run
Well then baby, keep on walkin'!

Too old for lies and head games
Never been a one night stand,
This lady has got too much to give
If you can't take it like a real man.

No more players, no more cheaters
Been there, ain't goin' back again,
I've had my share of losers
So, if you're not in it for the win-

Stop eye ballin' and your gawkin'
And I ain't fallin' for sweet talkin'
If you're not in it for the long run
Well then baby, keep on walkin'!

Because I'm lookin' for the real deal
Someone to be a lover and a friend,
I'll walk the line if you will too
And if you can't, well then you can-

Stop eye ballin' and your gawkin'
And I ain't fallin' for sweet talkin'
If you're not in it for the long run
Well then baby, keep on walkin'

If you're not in it for the long run…
Baby…keep on walkin'!

DÉJÀ VU

Out on Music Highway
The rides been long and hard-
I know where you've been
And I've been where you are.

I see you searching for traces
Of what's fallen behind-
Following destiny stone blinded
The way it is in your mind.

And I guess now you're wondering
Just how I knew?
Well my song is your song
Been there too…déjà vu !

I know it's lonely out there
When the roads been too long-
Searching for something
That might already be gone.

And when you're feeling lost
On Blues Avenue-
Keep straight on Dream Street
It's all mapped out for you!

And I guess now you're wondering
Just how I knew?
Well my song is your song
Been there too…déjà vu !

My song is your song
Take this one with you…
The rides long and hard
Been there too…déjà vu !

SMALL TOWN GIRL

Tess was a small town girl
With a guitar and big dreams,
Who wrote her own songs
And who liked to sing.

She spent days and nights
With pen and paper in hand,
To become a performer
Was her big career plan.

In a nine to five town
Built and made of tradition,
This wild child with a dream
Got little attention.

They said: Hey dream believer
You're a little speck in this world,
With far too big dreams
For a small hometown girl!

Tess kept writing and singing
No matter what they did say,
And she kept right on believing
She might make it someday.

She got a loan from the bank
And formed her own band,
And they went out on the road
In a big Chevy band.

Ten years have gone by now
And a couple gold records,
And as she sits in her studio
She sings out this message:

Hey small town dream believers
Little specks in this world,
Hold fast to your dreams
Follow your hearts boys and girls!

REBEL CHILDREN

There's been a lot said lately
About youth today gone wild,
Every time you turn around
There's another rebel child.

They're living in the cities
They're living in small towns,
They're screaming out to be heard
Yet, nobody hears a sound.

Have you ever felt looked down on?
Have you ever felt really scared?
Have you ever felt lost and alone-
And felt like no ones cares?

Tommy was just a young boy
When his Dad up and walked away,
And now his Mom works sixty hours a week
To keep the rent and the bills paid.
Tommy grew up fast and tough
Because the reality he found,
Survival is a constant struggle
On the poorer side of town.

But, Whitney, she was born to wealth
And had all that money can buy,
Except a Mom and Dad never home
Gave her an emptiness inside.
Whitney turned to booze and drugs
And things I will not mention,
Giving into lust mistook for love
Because it gave her some attention.

They're rich and they're poor

They're living in cities and small towns,
They're screaming out to be heard
Yet, nobody hears a sound.

Have you ever felt looked down on?
Have you ever felt really scared?
Have you ever felt lost and alone-
And felt like no one cares?

The rebel child needs a chance
They need a helping hand,
They need somebody to believe in them
They need somebody to understand-
They need not to be looked down on
They need not to be scared,
They need not to feel lost and alone
They need someone who cares!

They're screaming out to be heard-
Are you listening...do you care?

PHILOSOPHY OF A FLOWER CHILD

MY ALPHABET: AM FM LP CD VHS

MATH: Love + Music = Life Life-Music=Death

ENGLISH: The Rolling Stones, The Beatles, The Yardbirds, Queen, Led Zeppelin

SCIENCE: Inspiration>Creativity<Dreams>Believe=Music

HISTORY: I was born in 1957, my Mom said I was rockin' & rollin' in the womb to American Bandstand. The rest is history!

RELIGION: I looked faith up in the dictionary. It stated things such as: allegiance to duty or a person...loyalty and fidelity...believe in and trust in a higher power.

Sounds like a fan to me! Music is my religion!

PHILOSOPHY: The philosophy of this Flower Child is...everything I have ever needed to know came from music!

CREATIVE ART IS A HUMAN SERVICE

Elementary School:

What do you want to be when you grow up?

Ummm…a writer…write songs…sing with a band…work in a studio…maybe write a book…say stuff that helps people…make the world a better place!

High School:

Have you thought about your future?

Yeah man, I'm really in to writing and music and stuff. I want to make a difference in the world…help people…make them happy. Maybe like Bob Dylan or Joan Baez…stand up for something and sing it out…fight for freedom and social justice…songwriting and poetry and music is a really groovy way to do that…yeah, that would be really cool. Far out!

College:

When are you going to grow-up? You're not going to change the world writing poetry and song lyrics and banging on a drum! If you want to provide human services then you're going to have to get a real job!

Sigh…

Real Job:
Lisa, Human Services has been the perfect occupation for you! You've always been so aware of making positive change and helping people. Your caring and compassion have served you well. Your passion to provide advocacy and dedication to social justice is admirable.

I love my job!

And then I smile and giggle as I think:

You have no idea how many song lyrics and poems I have given people and hear them say: Me too! Exactly! That's how I feel! And how many people I've made feel better singing to them. I use my education to provide human services. I also use my heart and soul...creative arts is also a way to provide human service!

BYE, BYE, BABY BYE BYE

I'm cruising on down to the beach…windows open…CD blasting some Janis Joplin, The Queen Mother of Rock…in my book anyway. I'm belting it out and singing along…bye bye baby bye bye…my mind drift backs to the early 70's…

REHEARSAL:

In my neighborhood I am the lead singer in the band, tour manager, promoter, and public relations for the show. Today, like many days, I am transforming my neighbor's garage into a rock arena. I'm gathering up my background singers and trying to get them to take this show seriously, however, there appears to be alot of eye rolling and giggling and lack of dedication to my rock show! I loaded in with my microphone and RCA Victrola, and summoned my band, Debra, Karen, Alison, Catherine, Joanie, and my sister Lori, who runs sound.

"REHEARSAL LADIES!" I take the stage (otherwise known as the carpentry bench and storage area of the garage, which you have to climb up on using a garbage can as stairs to the stage) and we're ready to start. My sister drops the needle on the 45 spinning on the record player…and one, two, three, "You keep saying you got something for me, Something you call love but confess…" In the middle of the song, in the middle of rehearsal, my sister decides to take a break and is walking out of the arena. I stop rehearsal, and inquire: "Where are you going?" She replies she's hungry and is going home for lunch. "It's freaking rehearsal man…going home for lunch?" It appears she is a trend setter because my band is off the stage and going for lunch too! "Quitters!" Like I said they don't appear to have the passion and dedication for this band stuff!

SOUNDCHECK:

Everyone has had their lunch and hopefully a bit more serious about our rock show! Back up on stage we go, once again, Lori drops the needle on the 45, and one, two, three, I grab my mike, and "Billy Ray was a preacher's son." We run through a few more songs, sound is good, everyone appears to know what's going on. "OK gals, its cool, go do whatever you do, see you later for the show!" I get out some art paper and markers and make the tickets, the posters, and the programs for our rock show! Public Relations and Promotion!

SHOWTIME:

We get to stay up late tonight because of my rock show! And well, it's not a school night too. We still have to close before bedtime though. "What a drag, man!" We have a packed house!

Debra, Karen, Alison, Catherine, and Joanie, Lori ready to do sound, and mc, are peeking out from behind backstage with a case of the nerves and excitement of a rock band. At least I am! The neighborhood has gathered in lawn chairs, I mean the arena, including the two old cranky maidens from across the street that are always yelling at me to turn the music down! I knew they really liked me! My sister Lori takes the stage first and announces us: "Thank you for coming to my sister's dumb rock show, she made us do it!" Giggles from the crowd, and my back up singers! After the show Lori will be fired from running sound, and I will have a serious talk with these back up singers! It appears not everyone takes the music business as seriously as I do! My gals and I come out on stage, I grab my mic, and glare at my sister to drop the needle on the 45, and one, two, three, "You don't own me, I'm not one of your many toys." We are rocking the house!

ENCORE:

"...This is the way I always dreamed it would be..." dancing and singing band and crowd..."I can hear music...sweet, sweet, music..."

AFTER PARTY:

We load out and meet everybody in the driveway, I mean party hall, and I signed a few programs and tickets, drank Kool-Aid, and ate brownies and cookies. We thanked our fans for coming and partied until bedtime! "Living the dream!"

I'm cruising down to the beach…windows open…CD blasting some Janis Joplin…"bye bye baby bye bye…"

These Boots Are Made For Walkin': Nancy Sinatra
Son of a Preacher Man: Dusty Springfield
You Don't Own Me: Lesley Gore
I Can Hear Music: Ronnie Spector

CRY ME A RIVER

It was a rainy and windy night, and I was out with friends at the club rockin' to one of our favorite bands. I noticed a special weather report was making its way across the screen on the TV over the bar. There was a flash flood warning for our area and everyone was being instructed to use extra caution if driving on highways and secondary roads. Additionally, there were reports of trees and power lines down. I told my friend that was riding with me, we better head out, it might take us awhile to get home!

I dropped my friend at her place and carefully charted my way home. I drove very slowly as I already encountered fallen tree limbs, and downed power lines, and road closures. As I was approaching the highway, the bridge I needed to cross had raging rushing water below, however, just a bit on the road. I could still see the yellow line and felt it was safe to continue. The car ahead of me made it, so I proceeded to follow. I wasn't as lucky, and now understand, "flash flood!" DELUGE!!!! WALL OF WATER!!! Happens really fast!!! My car lifted up, I was washed off the bridge, and now headed downstream! I don't really have any recollection what was going through my mind, however, I did have the presence of mind to dial 911 on my cell phone, and help was on the way. My boat made by Chevrolet was now sinking and filling up with water fast. I grabbed my purse and my two cases of CD's from the passenger seat. I threw the CD's to the back window, as the weight of the engine was dragging the nose of the car down, and felt their best chance of survival was back there! MY best chance of survival right now was probably thinking about how to get out! I remembered stay in the car if you can as the current will drag you under and/or downstream, or if possible, get out on the roof, so the rescue workers can find you! Just as I was contemplating a plan, a rescue worker was beside the car! I don't know what made me look up at my visor, but there was one of my very favorite CD's: PRIDE & GLORY! I grabbed the CD and my purse as the rescue worker started to lift me out of the car. The rescue worker instructed me to hold my purse as he grabbed the CD and tried to throw it back into the car. As I put a death grip on Pride & Glory, I yelled: "Hey, this is Zakk Wylde! One of my favorite CD's!" The rescue worker replied: "I don't think Zakk Wylde gives a shit if you die in this river with his CD, so lets go!" So, I went! With my purse and PRIDE & GLORY, knowing it was going or they could pry it from my cold rigormortis hands!

At the Fire Station I was wrapped in warm blankets, drinking hot coffee, and waiting for my ride home, and the tow truck to rescue my car. The tow truck driver let me remove important documents from the glovebox of my car and handed me my two cases of CD's that also survived unscathed!

Once again, music plays a part in my survival!

Cry Me A River
~ZAKK WYLDE
Songwriter: Zakk Wylde

DREAM ON

Rocks! Here I am again! AEROSMITH in concert!

We are surrounded by some young kids thrilled to be seeing Aerosmith as we have been for many trips around the sun and many moons!

"Every time that I look in the mirror...All these lines on my face getting clearer...The past is gone...It went by like dusk to dawn..."

About mid concert, one of our young friends made an observation, and thinks its so cool an older lady like me is digging Aerosmith. I couldn't help myself, I responded: "Son, how the hell old do you think the band is?" I'm guessing my toys had been in the attic since before he was born! I was also thinking, great, now an old lady, not drinking, not smokin' dope, sober and straight, I am about to get in my first brawl at a rock concert! However, we both laughed, hugged, and bonded as Aerosmith fans!

My new young friend begged to hear stories from back in the day from myself and my friends, proud members of The Blue Army! I shared! He and his friends were beyond intrigued! This particular young man was also very interested in Aerosmith on LP...vinyl!!! I also shared my memories were not for sale, and there wasn't a price tag you could put on those LP's!

After the concert, my new young friend is following me out of the arena still bidding on my LP's! He's giving me his cell phone number, trying to take me out for a beer, whatever it takes! I turned to him and said: "DREAM ON!"

"Sing with me, sing for the year...Sing for the laughter and sing for the tear..."

Dream On
~AEROSMITH
Songwriter: Steven Tyler

THINGS MONEY CAN'T BUY

"…You know you got it if it makes you feel good…"
Piece of My Heart
~JANIS JOPLIN
Songwriters: Jerry Ragovoy/Bert Russell

There have been many mentors and muses along the way on my creative journey and life. As a young girl (and still!) these women were who I sang along with, inspired me, and I admired:
Ronnie Spector, Melanie, Buffy Sainte-Marie, Janis Joplin, Grace Slick, Chrissie Hynde,
Jackie DeShannon, Carole King, Carly Simon, Rita Coolidge, Tina Turner, Joan Jett,
Christine McVie, Nancy & Ann Wilson, Bonnie Tyler, Alanis Morrisette, Pat Benetar,
Bonnie Raitt, and many many more through the years…but, if I had to pick just one, from the 1970's to present… STEVIE NICKS!

I relate to Stevie Nicks on so many levels! Regarding her poetry, her songwriting, her spirit and witchy gypsy ways…I like to think I am one of the gypsies that remain!

I have been spilling feelings on to paper, pen in hand, since I can remember. Now through all the years, it remains my solace and celebration. No matter what I am going through, darkness or light, writing and music always brings me home. It has literally been my survival when all else may appear lost…pen in hand…feelings to paper…

The real reward and feeling of accomplishment are the "things money can't buy!"
When I share a piece of my heart… and see a tear in the eye, or hear a cry, or chocked up muffled sob…or see someone pointing to themselves nodding their head up and down, or the smile of solidarity, or sharing of laughter…priceless!

"…But I sing for the things money can't buy…"
I Sing for the Things
~STEVIE NICKS
Songwriter: Stevie Nicks

WALK THE WALK…TALK THE TALK

So, I need to tell you this story, to tell you the next one.

Besides a poet, lyric writer, whimsical wandering gypsy, and social activist, my real job is in human services. I am also an Empath and a Pisces, both a blessing and a curse. Fighting the system to help the under dog and folks in need has been my calling personally and professionally. For many years I worked the court system advocating for victims of domestic violence. I've also worked with teenage girls in the criminal justice system with addiction and mental health issues. I proudly served on The LGBT Task Force and remain an ally, and was a Legislative Liaison seeking more funds and resources for social services.

My rebel ways remain on and off the job! I like to feel I have walked the walk, not just talked the talk. I have worked one to three jobs at a time to survive most of my adult life. There is no shame in my game. I've hidden my vehicle after receiving a repossession letter, buying time until I could send the payment. I have survived the sheer panic of exiting a highway and turning and swerving on back roads after seeing a flatbed tow truck and dodging the repo-man! I've turned on the TV and discovered my cable was out…out until I had the money to pay the bill! I've come home and hit the light switch and remained in the dark…until I worked out a payment with the electric company! I've known the gamble of payday still being two days away and 1/8th of a tank of gas…my car has run on fumes and a miracle more times than I want to remember! Pay the bills or eat? I have known fasting and drastic dieting whether I wanted to or not!
Human Services allows me to work within the system to make the world a better place.
My creativity also allows me the freedom to do the same!

I have learned in my work and personally, what people need most is to be heard and validated!
People fighting their demons and needing resources basically just need someone to give a f#ck and a safe place to recover, without shame! As a society we have to STOP with the negativity and the stigma of depression,

anxiety, suicide, addiction, mental health issues, domestic violence, sexual abuse and assault, and how we identify! STOP! I try to be who I am professionally and personally. On the job or off I am "business casual!" Unlike my colleges I am definitely business casual! I am not the traditional looking suit and heels advocate. Look for me in dress jeans, a concert t-shirt, topped with casual suit jacket, with either leather boots or sandals, depending on the season! Perhaps a maxi dress or skirt…and I have a passion for long scarves and shawls. Somewhere between Stevie Nicks closet and Joe Perry's wardrobe trunk. I don't think it's a coincidence the rockers, free spirits, abused, bullied, addicted, depressed, suicidal, and lost souls, spill their guts to me. Spill their guts to me on the job and off! I am one of those people complete strangers sit next to and tell me the stories of their life!

Then came the day I had to practice what I preached!

I thought I walked the walk and talked the talk…and I did! However… helping others was a great distraction from dealing with my own demons! I had long dealt with low self-esteem and self-worth. I knew I had high functioning anxiety and felt I hid it well and dealt with it. I've had issues with eating disorders and being a perfectionist. I have been in and out of unhealthy relationships and experienced abandonment issues and would soon learn I had codependency and PTSD issues too! ALL very carefully repressed focusing on helping others! Staying busy and flying by the seat of my pants lifestyle = trauma response!

Professionally, I did my job and did it well!

Personally, I did it well…until I didn't! It was time to help myself…it was time to walk my walk and talk my talk!

TIMES LIKE THESE

"…And here's to the lost and lonely dreamers…
Struggling to survive…"
Lonely Dreamers
STEPPENWOLF
Songwriters: John Kay/Rocket Ritchotte

PLAY:

The Rolling Stones, Queen, Led Zeppelin, The Yardbirds, The Beatles, Steppenwolf, The Doors, The Byrds, The Band, Bob Dylan, John Prine, Graham Parsons, Donavan, Creedence Clearwater Revival, Aerosmith, Eagles, Fleetwood Mac, J Giels Band, Jeff Healy, Tom Petty & The Heartbreakers, Bob Seeger, John Cougar Mellencamp, Bruce Springsteen… on to the 80's, 90's and beyond…

PAUSE/STOP:

I was late to the table when Foo Fighters was being served!

I loved their music and knew they were one of the greatest bands in rock n' roll, but, I didn't know any of their songs beginning to end.

Now…laying on a table in a hospital emergency triage, with a crisis counselor in attendance, I was about to hit Replay! The crisis counselor asked me in what ways could I soothe myself? I answered her…MUSIC! Music has always served as my survival, and right now laying here suicidal…I was trying hard to survive. What I was really trying to decide was whether to survive or not! She nodded, left the room, and came back with a portable CD Player, headphones, and a handful of CD's. I grabbed Foo Fighters, Skin and Bones, and hit Play. It was right about here…"It's times like these you learn to live again…," Foo Fighters got my full attention! However, the crisis counselor wanted my attention…hit Pause. I shared my story with her how my life had been rough for years. Too many years working two and three jobs at a time to survive. Music has always been my passion, but I had enough trouble keeping the rent paid, lights on, gas in my car, and time and money for music was few and far between. I had been a writer most of my life, however, my poems and song lyrics had long ago seen the light of day and were buried in a box. Being in and out of unhealthy relationships dragged me down too. All of the above…was how I ended up here, on this table, in emergency triage. Too many years of loss, most of all I lost "me!" I have forgotten who "I" was and didn't have time "to be" even if I remembered. The crisis counselor excused herself again and again promised to be right back. I hit Play! She returned with a journal, and I kept listening to Foo Fighters and her at the same time. On the first page of the journal she wrote: "Instead of why is this happening to me, choose, what am I supposed to learn from this?" She thought since I enjoyed creative writing, keeping a journal would help me express myself. Well, fuck that! If I knew the answer to that, I wouldn't be here! I tuned her out and turned up Foo Fighters…"I am a little divided, Do I stay or run away, And leave it all behind…" Wait! What?

REWIND & REPLAY

I spent the next few days deciding whether to stay or run away. I pondered why is this happening to me and what was I supposed to learn from this. I hit play and replay on YouTube and CD's. I hit play and replay on everything Foo Fighters, songs, stories, and interviews. And that journal… that journal was the beginning of note taking that became this book you're reading right now! My hope is my story might help somebody else in their story. As for the Foo Fighters…Times Like These will forever remain my fight song! When I feel a little divided, I remind myself times like these you learn to live again, to give again, to love again…time and time again! I am a bonafide fan and eternally grateful!

Times Like These
FOO FIGHTERS
Songwriters: Dave Grohl/Taylor Hawkins/Nate Mendel/Chris Shiflett

Recovery

DISCLAIMER: This portion of the book is not intended to be, or to be considered, as expert advice or counsel.

This is my experience. This is my recovery. This is my journey and served as a cathartic release the best way I know how…creative writing.

I use the word "HE" when describing "the abuser" because that was my experience. It can happen in any relationship and any gender you may identify as or partner with.

DOMESTIC VIOLENCE as I understand it is about power and control. Stereotypically, we are often taught to believe domestic violence or abuse in relationships is physical. It is! It is also verbal abuse, emotional abuse, psychological abuse, sexual abuse, financial abuse, and spiritual abuse.

NARCISSISTIC ABUSE as I understand it is all of the above, however, an animal all of its own!

Basically, a Narcissist is the most self-absorbed, grandiose, arrogant, and self-righteous individual, you will ever encounter! They seek constant attention and adoration, and are emotionally, psychologically, spiritually, and physically, exhausting! They are experts at "gas-lighting" and driving you crazy! The typical narcissistic man will present as Prince Charming. He is the spider to the fly! Charming until he has you in his web, and then you will be caught up in his destruction. He will destroy you!

Hello, my name is Lisa, and I am Codependent!

Codependency is an unhealthy relationship with another, putting their feelings, their needs, and their issues, before your own. People pleasing! Poor at setting boundaries, and feeling responsible for fixing the other person! Seeks validation from others. Lacks self-esteem and self-worth. As a Codependent I felt I was acting out of love. What I learned was, I didn't know how to stop loving! I had to learn to love myself first and separate myself from unhealthy relationships. You can't make someone take responsibility for their behaviors if they don't think they need to change or want to change. The ONLY person you can change is yourself.

With counseling and support groups and a lot of surrendering and acceptance...I am healing.

No more shame! I am learning to live with high functioning anxiety, PTSD issues, eating disorder issues and codependency issues. I am a work in progress every day. I own it!

I also work hard to be a strong advocate for not letting shame and the stigma of mental health issues stop myself or others for seeking support and help.

Tell your story! Tell your story so somebody else can tell theirs!

RECOVERY

My first unhealthy relationship with a man was with my Dad. He was a good provider and a hard worker but emotionally unavailable. I believe he had undiagnosed mental health issues. I now understand through my own recovery he couldn't give what he didn't have. I now understand he projected his demons on to my Mom, my sister, and to me, and we all coped in our own ways. I learned at a young age to walk on eggshells and live on high alert and to keep things pleasing in hopes to keep peace. I also learned at this same young age not to talk about what goes on behind closed doors and learned the art of pretending everything was alright. Repress the fear…repress the hurt…repress the shame!

When all hell broke loose as it often did, I retreated. My saving grace was music and my own creativity of writing poems and short stories. I would lock myself in my room and listen to music. Music and song lyrics created a happy place where all was well…it also provided me a voice in sad songs, dark songs, that gave the feeling of not being alone, and someone else understands.

Often, I would leave the house and go to my secret hiding place of solace. A small open area in the woods behind the house. My transistor radio would provide music of peace and harmony, as did writing down my feelings on notebook paper, sometimes making my feelings rhyme like my favorite songs! My favorite instrument to play was two sticks and a flat rock…drumming felt calming and soothing. Drums are still my favorite instrument for pleasure, and also very therapeutic for me as one of my modalities of mental health care! Obviously, so is music and writing and spilling my guts on paper!

I took care of my Dad in his final days and cared for him right up to his last breath, and I would do it again. There was no grand closure, no emotional deathbed goodbye, just acceptance.

For everything he wasn't, he was still my Dad, and I understand he did the best he could.

Barely home from our honeymoon and living in a mobile home at the time, he decided we were getting a puppy. I decided we were not! Both of us working full time jobs and living in a confined space wasn't fair to the dog! I lost the argument (as per usual) I never had much to say about anything...and the puppy arrived. Not the puppy's fault at all, but, so began the battles of whose turn it was to clean up the puppy poop. The following incident should have been enough to send me packing right then and there! But it would be ten more years before I made that move. One night during the puppy poop battles I lost the battle regarding who was going to clean up the puppy poop. He grabbed me by my hair on the back of my head, knocked me to the floor, and shoved my face in the puppy poop! My punishment for not following orders! I got up and cleaned myself up, and dutifully cleaned up the puppy poop. Right to this day I remember the humiliation and gut wrenching feeling of helplessness and being controlled! Before I could follow through on an escape plan there was a baby on the way and a home to take care of.

I made the best of the next few years telling only my close friends what was going on. There were some good times, but the scale always tipped more in the opposite direction. I fulfilled my role as wife and mother, he played the role of have your cake and eat it too! He did whatever he wanted (and did!) I did what I was told to do! He literally controlled where I went, who I saw, and what I was allowed to do! My friends still remember I could only talk on the phone when he wasn't home, and they were afraid to visit me, because they didn't want me to pay the price of disobeying! Parties, bars, his buddies, and a fondness for young women were his priorities. Then there was a wife and child for social appearances when needed. No matter what time he chose to come home, dinner was waiting! Sometimes, one or two in the morning, I arose from the bed, went to the kitchen, warmed and served his dinner!

He had a reputation as a bully growing up and was infamous for his bad temper! I knew this when we were dating, and had several reservations before tying the knot, but I believed he would change with love. NOT!

I was about to implement another plan of escape with my daughter when my whole world was rocked! He made a confession and let loose a secret past, that didn't remain a secret, as it was scandalized in the newspapers and evening news! Again, I played the role of dutiful wife through his court hearings and incarceration, all in front of a relentless media circus! I had the hope that when he returned home, he would get the mental health care he needed. I also started to realize that shame shouldn't stop people from getting help! I believe if he had received the help he needed in his childhood, his life might have turned out different…and mine! It was also a good paradigm of my codependency. However, it would be years before I knew what that was, and I was one! Codependent! Just as in my childhood, I thought I had control of the situation and could make everything alright! Anyway…nothing changed! He showed no remorse, made no restitution, and was happy to live his life and freely carry on! One year later I finally called it quits! There was a flurry of lawsuits connected to his crime and during the divorce process my daughter and myself, lost everything. We lost our home, material possessions, and money. We left ground zero and started over. He went on with his life, per usual, parties, bars, buddies, and a fondness for young women. I carried on a single Mom, working two-three jobs to survive, and my daughter and I lived with the trauma, shame, and paying the cost of a crime we didn't commit! Through recovery I am coming to terms with how much this all cost me…mentally, physically, financially, and psychologically! One of my best friends from childhood has often remarked: "It was painfully obvious!" The real tragedy of this story, was how different our lives would have all been had he got the help he needed growing up! His life would have been happier too! I believe with all my heart, the love remained, as a matter of fact, it's a sad love story. He made things right in the end, and I hope he is resting in peace.

I've never gotten a relationship right! My codependency, abandonment issues, low self-worth and self-esteem issues, trauma and PTSD issues, didn't know how to have a healthy relationship.

Then, I met Prince Charming! Prince Charming who my counselor thought to be a dry drunk with serious narcissistic issues, who literally kicked me to the curb! I have learned there is not much of a chance for a narcissist seeking recovery, because they will never think or believe they have a problem, or anything is wrong with what they do and who they are!

So…kicked to the curb and to a stretcher in emergency triage with a crisis counselor! Let recovery begin…

LOVE WILL CHANGE HIM

Many did warn me-
Girl, it won't last,
He'll use you and lose you
Just like the girls in his past!
(But my love will change him!)

He'll lie and he'll cheat-
Your feelings he'll trash,
He shows no remorse
For the hearts broken in the past!
(But my love will change him!)

Many did warn me-
Girl, it won't last,
He'll use you and lose you
Just like the girls in his past!
(But my love will change him!)

Now, I'm out on the street
Thrown out on my ass,
Guess, it's true what they say
About you and your past!
(My love didn't change him!)

AS MY CODEPENDENT WORLD SPINS

Here I am!
Right back where I've been,
Turned up, down, and inside out
As my codependent world spins.

I can't take this anymore!
It's either sink or swim,
Swim and try to save me
Or sink while saving him.

He's not changing me!
And I'm not changing him,
The craziness continues
As my codependent world spins.

I can't take this anymore!
It's either me or him,
Do I let go and change myself
Or hold on to changing him?

So, here I am!
As my codependent world spins,
Learning the only thing I can change-
Is myself and my codependence.

WALKING THE FLOOR

Night after night…I can't take any more!

Your cruel words never end
Night after night after night,
No matter how hard I try
I don't do anything right!

I reach for a hug
You show me your fist,
You love me, you hate me
I don't deserve this!

I don't make enough money
I'm not enough fun,
Now matter how much I do
Nothing is done!

I'm too boring and quiet
I talk way too much,
I'm not home when I'm needed
I don't work enough!

I'm way too possessive
I don't care about you,
What in the hell
Do you want me to do?

I reach for a hug
You show me your fist,
You love me, you hate me
I don't deserve this!

Your cruel words never end
Night after night after night,

No matter how hard I try
I don't do anything right.

Night after night...until I walked out the door!

THE LAST TIME

The last time I saw you
Is the last time I'll see you
Said the note she left on the door-
And the last time I left here
It won't be the same
Because I'm not coming back anymore!

She packed up her pride, her heart, and possessions
Walked down the stairs and out the front door,
No more one more chance, no more one last try
No more coming back like before!

He couldn't believe the words she wrote
So he read it again once more,
The last time I left here, it won't be the same-
Because I'm not coming back anymore!

No more one last chance
No more one last try
No more coming back like before-
And the last time he saw her
Was the last time he saw her
Just like she said in the note on the door!

RECIPE FOR DISASTER

INGREDIENTS

CODEPENDENT EMPATH
- open, honest, heart on sleeve
- seeks security
- low self-worth
- insecure
- anxious, highly emotional
- always seeking approval
- communication is key
- constantly apologizing
- gives to the point of exhaustion
- crying, feeling crazy

-NARCISSIST
- emotionally unavailable
- impulsive
- self-absorbed
- grandiose
- gas lighter, control freak
- master manipulator
- silent treatment
- plays victim and martyr
- never satisfied taker
- tormentor

MIX

I'm sorry!
It hurts me when you do that!
I am upset!
I'm feeling confused!
I live here too!
I have a right to speak!
We need to communicate!

It's all your fault!
It's all in your head!
You're crazy!
You need to shut up!
This is MY house!
You'll do what your told!
Smirk and silent treatment!

SERVES

Nobody!!!!!!!!!!!

STORE & KEEP

Recovery & Awakening!
Lesson!

No remorse! Remains the same!
Moves on to next victim!

A NARCISSIST WEAPONS OF DESTRUCTION
(My Personal Experience With One!)

SMIRK: Smiles Maliciously In Response Kinglike!

GASLIGHTING: Does something right in front of you, or says something, then denies it ever happened…crazy making!

BAIT AND SWITCH: Promises Prince Charming, delivers Dr. Jekyll-Mr. Hyde

MASTER MANIPULATOR: Thrives on creating drama! Thrives on creating confusion and insecurity, then blames it on you when you react and calls you crazy!

SUPERIORITY AND GRANDOISE: Believes he is smarter than most. Con Artist at best! Only cares about himself and will drain you physically, mentally, and financially, without giving back. If you stop holding him up on his pedestal you will be easily dispensable!

INTIMIDATION: Non-verbal intimidation was when he would display his handgun that was always readily available in his boot holster!

Verbal: Constant emotional and psychological abuse!

POWER AND CONTROL: Gaining your trust to be vulnerable and trusting and open with your feelings and then using all your vulnerabilities against you as weakness and making you believe you are "less than" and crazy!

Portrays Mr. Nice Guy image so no one will believe you when you tell what is going on behind closed doors! Creates dependency!

PROJECTION: Places his own toxic traits on to you! Blames you for his actions, feelings, or what he says! Makes you feel sorry for him when HE caused harm!

MR PAIN

What started out love and light
Ended dark and distained,
Living with Dr. Jekyll-Mr. Hyde
Under the rule of his domain.

Prince Charming was just a lie
Your smoke and mirrors and head games,
It appears your modus operandi
Knows no remorse or shame.

Just like the one before me
Who you ridiculed and defamed,
Now I'm the one not good enough
For Mr. Victim, Mr. Vain!

Everything you loved and respected about me
Became my ball and chain,
My social activism, My free spirit
Now you want me to change.

Well, you're not who you presented to be
The loyal gentleman you claimed,
There were many red flags and warnings
But I believed you just the same.

Gaslighting and crazy making
You almost drove me insane,
While you played Prince Charming
Dr. Jeckell-Mr. Hyde…Mr. Pain!

PROVE ME WRONG

Here's my story and I'm sticking to it
No more falling in love-Be gone!
I think I find the right one-
Then he proves to me I'm wrong!

I'm down to my last broken heart
Trusting love and getting fooled-
I've given all that I can give
And lost all that I can lose!

Don't believe in fairy tales
Truth is the Prince is lying,
There's no happily ever after
In the end he'll leave you crying!

He'll leave you with a broken heart
He'll leave you feeling like a fool-
Taking all that you can give
And all that you can lose!

That's my story and I'm sticking to it
No more falling in love-Be gone!
But somewhere hidden between the lines
I hope someone proves me wrong!

...I f he is the right one
He will prove me wrong!

GLAD I SURVIVED

She was a free spirit
With nothing to hide,
The sky was the limit
Each day of her life.

Then she was shot down
Deeply wounded inside,
Like a broken winged bird
That could no longer fly.

The fall seemed unbearable,
The pain made her cry,
She knew she'd live through it
But she wanted to die.

Each day she was healing
She'd look towards the sky,
Could this wounded free spirit
Give life one more try?

She had been shot down
Slowly healing inside,
But the broken winged bird
Would once again fly!

The fall seemed unbearable
The pain made her cry,
But the sky is the limit-
I'M glad I survived.

FREE SPIRIT STYLE

Once upon a time
Carefree and versatile,
I was satisfied heart and soul
In my free spirit style.

I knew who I was inside and out
I knew what I wanted to do,
I knew love and light
And life was kinda cool!

What happened to my heart and soul?
My free spirit style?
Once upon time
Carefree and versatile?

I lost myself inside and out
I didn't know what to do,
Darkness shadowed love and light
And life was kinda cruel!

I learned to navigate the darkness
When life's dark and kinda cruel,
I learned about myself inside and out
Now I know what to do!

Recovery saved me heart and soul!
I'm again carefree and versatile!
One day at a time
In my free spirit style!

AT PEACE & STRONG

Your constant abuse and many lies
Just about did me in,
You almost drove me crazy
In the hell that I lived in.

But everything is alright now
Now that you are gone,
You can't hurt me anymore
I am at peace & I am strong!

No more abuse and no more lies
I walked out of hell today,
My life is mine again
I'm going to be okay.

Everything is alright now
Now that you are gone,
You can't hurt me anymore
I am at peace & I am strong!

NOT HURT ANYMORE

With my pen in my hand
Mightier than your sword,
I release the heartache
I'm not hurt anymore.

No more broken heart!
No more walking the floor!
No more sobbing and crying!
No more being ignored!
No more of your crazy making!
No more slamming doors!
No more of your head games!
No more cut to the core!
No more trying to change you!
No more me screaming until hoarse!
No more of your anger and threats!
No more you…anymore!

With my pen in my hand
Mightier than your sword,
I release the heartache
I'm not hurt anymore!

NOT BROKEN ANYMORE

Another night in hell! Pushing, shoving, and verbal assault was not enough this time, he went for my record collection! At first, I thought it was just a threat, just more of the usual mind-fuck. Then there it was!
Snap! Pop! Crack! Broken!
One of my favorite albums. It had survived over thirty years and many seasons of my life, now destroyed in one minute, by one asshole!
Then a second one!
Snap! Pop! Crack! Broken!

I literally dropped to my knees crying and begging. I pleaded with him to stop! To add to his drama, he starts chanting in sing-song voice: "One, two, three, four, lets have some fun and break some more!" He followed by making fun of my poetry and making fun of my songwriting! He took the rhymes of some songs I wrote and mocked and ridiculed! Amusing himself he sings:
"How do you like my poems, poet? Listen to my rhymes sing!"

And then...
Snap! Pop! Crack! Broken!
Another record gone...

I curled up on the floor in a ball! He's happy now! He's broken me too!

I got up, and ran up the stairs to the bedroom, locking the door behind me. He followed me! Behind the locked door I hear him. He's laughing in sarcasm and then I hear...
Snap! Pop! Crack! Broken!

He shouts at me through the door: "Hey rock star, get your notebook out and write one about me, dedicate it to me, so when your rich and famous I will be famous too!"

I heard his footsteps go down the stairs. From behind the locked door, I sobbed in response:

"I will!"

He's out of my life now! My music and writing are mine again! I'm no longer broken!

And…by request:

"One, two, three, four, This ones for you and I got more, One, two, three, four,
You're famous now and evermore, One, two, three, four, I'm not broken anymore!"

POETIC JUSTICE
(Relapse!)

A short story about my codependent relapse.

A musician, and a legend in his own mind. This guy had a set list worth of every woman I ever been with done me wrong songs! Additionally, enough sad stories to fill a self-help section of any bookstore about his life of misfortune, none of it his fault! It is with bemused embarrassment I confess I fell for most of it!

Both of us being creative people, I shared my poetry and song lyrics with him, showing him my creative being. He thought they were mediocre, but, had potential. He would try and correct and revise my creative works to make them what he thought people might consider good. However, he warned me they were not marketable. His humble professional opinion!

Personally, I had work to do also! He told me if we were going to date, he was concerned about what people would think of him dating "a fatty!" I was instructed to lose some weight and make some other minor adjustments! He had his public image to uphold, I guess! Both of us were in our sixties, and neither one of us were exactly centerfold models!

Mind you, he had no problem with my pocketbook! I handed out gas money, cigarette money, and spending cash on a weekly basis! I bought groceries, financed day trips, dinners, drinks, and gigs! My pocketbook he fully approved of!

After about four or five weekends I did recognize my part in this! Codependent relapse!

Codependent relapse at its finest!

Time to go! Good-bye! It was now I found out about his criminal record for domestic violence, and other con man scams! Probably wasn't the best advocate for MY self- improvement, or reliable source for every woman I've been with done me wrong songs, and sad stories of a life of misfortune!

Hi I'm Lisa and I'm Codependent!

Just a short story about my codependent relapse with a con man, and perhaps a bit of poetic justice!

YOU'LL NEVER BE LISA

(With all due respect to one of my favorite songwriters:
Jessi Colter, I wrote my own Lisa song)

You'll never be Lisa
You were told long ago,
But your ego and arrogance
Just would not let go.

You sold your soul, girl!
But, love always wins-
And as we all know
Truth comes out in the end!

Love bought and traded
With material things,
All quite impressive
But with attached strings.

You sold your soul, girl!
But, love always wins-
And as we all know
Truth comes out in the end!

Your façade love story
Made for a good show,
But you'll never be Lisa
You were told long ago.

You sold your soul, girl!
But, love always wins-
And as we all know
Truth comes out in the end!

I OWN IT

So…I live my life one day at a time. A work in progress. Surrendering… Accepting…Healing.

I own it!

I remain a firm believer and advocate of tell your story so somebody else can tell theirs.

I'm not sure what is up ahead or around the next corner, but I am sure of this:

No person, no material possession, no amount of money…is worth more than your self-esteem, self-expression, or the freedom to be yourself!

Warrior Spirit

DIVINE INTERVENTION

Spirit will send the right people to you. Spirit will guide your way if you pay attention!

You will connect soul to soul with these people. You will be free to be yourself with complete abandon and live fearlessly in your truth.

Let go of the illusion of control. If your path is blocked or wishes denied, you are being redirected on your chosen path. You will understand as you journey on.

Spirit will put people in your path that were not good for you. Those people were lessons! Spirit will let you get lost from time to time, so you can find yourself!

I have made a lot more meaningful relationships sharing my struggles, than I ever did through trying to be what society deems successful and acceptable. I have discovered my destiny by being lost, through the hills and valleys, and having to map my way to where I was meant to be, not necessarily the straightest or easiest path.

Allow Divine Intervention to show you the way. Synchronicity is a message, not a coincidence, that's divine intervention at work. That fluke of good luck, that chance meeting, that's serendipity, that's the miracle of divine intervention. Trust it.

MY REPURPOSED HEART

At a retreat exploring grief and healing, I created a heart made of repurposed clay.

With the idea of repurposed in mind, meaning making something different, out of something that once was something else, our task was to create art that represented loss and healing in our life. The facilitator shared: "Grief is just love with no place to go." Loss and love with no place to go drove me to suicidal ideation and a breakdown just a year ago, so I created my repurposed heart.

Our next assignment was to take our creation of repurposed art and release it back to the earth from whence it came, also releasing our loss and grief to the universe, for healing.

As divine intervention would have it, I already had another retreat planned the following weekend! I would be staying in a small wooden bungalow in the forest. Without hesitance or any reservation, I thought it was the perfect resting place for my repurposed heart.

I arrived and settled into my bungalow. First to the forest with my repurposed heart, and then later in the evening a sound meditation. I have been to this retreat many times, and done an enormous amount of healing here, so again, divine intervention at work! I walked the familiar path up the hill by the ledge, and down the hill along the meadow. My repurposed heart still in hand, I again, walked up the path by the ledge, and circled back around down the path along the meadow. My repurposed heart still in hand, I was having a difficult time letting it go!

I decided to take it back to the bungalow with me and began to walk the path back. I walked along the path, across the natural rock bridge over a little babbling stream, and the resting place for my repurposed heart found me! I thanked Spirit for showing me the resting place for my repurposed heart and released it.

In celebration, I enjoyed a forest bath, and feasted on cheese and fruit and crackers, and a glass of wine.

The sound meditation was beyond enchanting!

In the forest, laying on a natural bed of moss, under a starlit sky with a waning moon, the gongs and the chimes had me floating between the earth and the sky! While in deep meditation I thought about my repurposed heart now at rest, and how I was anxious when I was having a difficult time finding its resting place, and how I was finally able to let it go and felt closure and peace. Guided by the gongs and chimes, and Spirit, my human heart skipped a beat and tears ran down my cheeks. It had been that simple all along! All I ever had to do was let it go. All my losses in life were lessons of things not meant to be. When walking my path and feeling anxious and unsure, stop trying so hard and the answer will come in its own time.

So onward I go, with a lesson from my repurposed heart…

I created my new path in life, making something different out of something that once was…and when grief and loss come along, and it will…find a place for that love to go.

THANKFUL LOSER
(Thank you to Rob DeSorbo for the inspiration)

I am a thankful loser
Because I finally understand,
The losses and the blessings
Are all part of the grand plan.

I am now grateful for my losses
And things not meant to be,
I know Spirit has a greater plan
And it will be shown to me.

I will be bold yet empathetic
I will emanate love and light,
However, knowing how to set boundaries
Self-respect first, without contrite.

I will stop, look, and listen
And be grateful for every day,
I trust without a doubt
Spirit will guide the way.

I am a thankful loser
Because I finally understand,
The losses and the blessings
Are all part of the grand plan.

ALONG THE PATH OF LIFE

I cannot change my yesterdays
Old regrets or past mistakes,
But I'm in charge of my tomorrows
I'm the Ms. of my fate.
Along the path of life, I stumbled
Lost my way and fell,
Up and down the roads of yesterday
I saw my share of hell!
Many lessons to be learned
Too many learned the hard way,
But through it all right or wrong
I'm better off today.
I keep growing with experience
And I'm learning all the time-
Take the good and carry on
And leave the bad behind.

WHITE WITCH

I practice yoga and meditation
And nature bathing too,
I believe in the power of Goddess
Healing herbs and organic foods.

I live by the Law of Three
What you put out comes back to you!
I draw power from the moon
And the sea and rivers too.

Peace, love, and light
Is the magic that I use,
Lessons from the cosmos
My Book of Shadows too.

I practice this life with pure intention
There's no evil in my craft,
A modern pagan often misunderstood
Just like my Sisters in the past.

It was just a few centuries ago
Our kind were banished and ridiculed,
At Gallows Hill, in Massachusetts
In 1692.

BLUE MOON

It's the mojo bag of nights
The mystical Blue Moon!
If you believe in magic
In the enchantment of full moons.

Cast a spell with harm to none
Pure intention and white light,
Make a wish upon a star
The Blue Moon is mojo night.

Trusting in the Law of Three
Use practical magic with love,
What goes around comes around
Just like the universe does.

If you believe in magic
In the enchantment of full moons,
It's the mojo bag of nights
The mystical Blue Moon!

MERMAID

Once upon a time I was a mermaid
In the sea way down below,
Tales and sea-lore tell about us
But only mermaids really know.

Only mermaids know the real story
Of life way down below the sea,
For centuries we've kept our secret
Sisters of The Mermaid Society.

However, yes, we have been seen
By folks in schooners, boats, and ships,
And yes, for sure my human friends
We really do exist!

We've been known to swim ashore
Our favorite time, full moons,
And together sit upon the rocks
Melodiously singing mermaid tunes.

Next time you're by the ocean
On some warm summer night,
You may hear our sweet songs
Or maybe see us in the moonlight.

Tales and sea-lore tell about us
But only mermaids really know,
Once upon I was a mermaid
In the sea way down below.

FOREST NYMPH

As far back as I can remember the forest was my safe place...my happy place.

When all hell was breaking loose in the real world, all was calm and magical, in my forest world! I loved the solitude of my peaceful place and would gather flowers and other offerings making alters and rooms. It was my own enchanted land! I would twirl and dance, and sing songs, and journal creative writing in my notebooks, and drum on rocks with sticks. I enjoyed being with other children but looking back I was kind of a loner. Little did I know then I was a free spirit and forest nymph in training!

The forest is still my safe place...my happy place.

I can twirl and dance, sing songs, write my poems and song lyrics, and play my drums!

When all hell is breaking loose in the real world...I find solace in my forest world.

Still a free spirit...still a forest nymph!

ODE TO MY FRAME DRUM

(In Memory of: Layne Redmond)

When the drummers were women
Divine Feminine sung-
Spiritual communion
Body, mind, and the drum.

With every beat of my heart
And drums rhythmic sound-
Cosmic consciousness awakes
As harmony propounds.

Great Goddesses before me
Of long ago-
I feel your cadence connection
In my heart and my soul.

We women drummers today
Keep Divine Feminine sung-
A solidarity of Sisterhood
In body, mind, and the drum.

UPSIDE OF DOWN

(In Memory of: Bill Chace)

Been battered and broken
Been turned upside down-
Things sure as hell better
On the upside of down!

Times I've been crazy
Now, I've turned life around-
Getting it together
On the upside of down!

I've made my decision
True love turned me around-
Life's sure as hell better
On the upside of down!

Bill and I became friends through music and...similar lives! I remember when he called me so excited that he met his soulmate Nancy! The last time I saw him, just weeks before he died, we had revisited how great life had been for him since they had been together. He said it felt so good to live on the upside of down. I told him that sounded like a good line for a song! He told me to take it and run with it.

Our mutual love was for a band he managed for years: DIAMONDBACK! I would be remiss if I didn't express my love, gratitude, and inspiration to this band:

DIAMONDBACK: Jeff Wheeler, Jeff Alamed, Paul Lusky, and memory of Paul Bassett.

Also: Jimi Bell, BJ Zampa & Clark Denis.

And to some lovely ladies I also had the pleasure to spend this time of my life with:

Nancy Fraga, Sandy Wheeler, Brenda Bassett, and Michelle Denis.

FUCKING CRAZY

Being a trauma survivor sucks! PTSD sucks! Anxiety and Depression sucks! Addictions suck!

People calling us crazy really sucks!

But, We, "fucking crazy" have survived more than I hope you ever have to experience!

Survivors! We "fucking crazy" are survivors!

In my darkest hours I have learned to hold on to the return of the light. In my times of light, I have learned to hold the light for those finding their way through the darkness. Like the ones who held the light for me.

My "fucking crazy" is right here in the pages of this book, in the spotlight, because this "fucking crazy" never wants you to feel "fucking crazy" alone!

This "fucking crazy" is going to try to keep shining, keep loving, and keep caring!

This "fucking crazy" is grateful for the ones who shared their "fucking crazy" and gave me a voice!

Survivors! We "fucking crazy" are survivors!

Being a trauma survivor sucks! PTSD sucks! Anxiety and Depression sucks! Addictions Suck!

People calling us crazy really sucks!

WHERE THE RIVER FLOWS

Someday when I leave this world
When to the Summerland I go,
I hereby make this last request-
Put me where the river flows.

Put me where the river flows
Set my spirit free,
Let love and light-peace and harmony
Be my legacy.

I hereby make this last request
When to the Summerland I go,
Someday when I leave this world
Put me where the river flows!

Put me where the river flows
Set my spirit free,
Let love and light-peace and harmony
Be my legacy.

When to the Summerland I go...
Put me where the river flows.

LEGACY

Someday when I leave this world
My warrior spirit free-
Let love and light, and a humble life
Be my legacy.

To the Summerland I will go
But in your heart, I will stay-
If you look for me in these simple things
I'll never be far away.

I'm the shooting star and Pisces constellation
I'm the sunbeams and the moonglow-
I'm the gentle rain and falling snowflakes
I'm the storm and I'm the rainbow.

I'm the waves out on the ocean
I'm the waterfall and bubbling stream-
I'm the worn dirt road and forest path
I'm a wildflower hill and valley ravine.

I'm the cricket and the tree toad songs
I'm the howling wolf and seagull scream-
I'm the chattering woodland creatures
I'm the whale, the starfish, and water breams.

Yes, to the Summerland I will go
But in your heart, I will stay-
If you look for me in these simple things
I'll never be far away.

So, someday when I leave this world
My warrior spirit free-
Let love and light, and a humble life
Be my legacy.

WARRIOR SPIRIT

So, this is the end of my book, but not the end of my story!

I will carry on with my journey as a Warrior Spirit. A non-violent fighting warrior of love and light, and social justice.

Reflection, Redemption, and Recovery, helped me heal from the challenges and adversity I have encountered so far. With a warrior spirit I still struggle with some bumps in the road that trigger reminders of dead ends and burned bridges. However, I have learned to use those reminders as speed bumps, or a detour to use caution and map out a better way. As a warrior spirit I want to serve as a companion for others who may have fallen or lost their way along their journey. I hope to drive all that passion home with courage and humility, as I empower myself and as empowerment for others.

I remain grateful to the warrior spirits before me that shared their stories and gave me a voice to share mine.

NATIONAL DOMESTIC VIOLENCE HOTLINE   800 799 7233

SUICIDE AND CRISIS LIFELINE   988

SUPPORT FOR ADDICTION TREATMENT   800 839 1686

DEAR TO MY HEART!
MUSICARES 800 687 4227
MusiCares Development
3030 Olympic Blvd.
Santa Monica, CA 90404

DUEL DIAGNOSIS
www.dueldiagnois.com

INDEX

ABOUT THE AUTHOR

LISA ALLEN THOMPSON is the quintessential warrior spirit! Her passions are, the love of nature, music and song, playing her hand drums, and philosophy. She believes every living thing is part of the circle of life, and respect for the entity is key to survival. She promotes compassion and is an ardent advocate for social justice.

Lisa lives in Connecticut, however, she feels at home at many of her favorite places throughout New England. Her creative works have been published in many newspapers and journals, and well received at public appearances.

Printed in the United States
by Baker & Taylor Publisher Services